D0062132

MEMORIES OF A GOLDEN AGE

Courtesy of the Historic New Orleans Collection, Detail, Acc. No. 1982.96

Memories of a Golden Age

A GLIMPSE INTO THE RIVER REGION PAST

JOANNE AMORT

2 0 0 0

OAK ALLEY FOUNDATION

VACHERIE, LOUISIANA

This book is not an academic history. It is a story based on history. As such we trust that we have made fair use of available resource materials.

COPYRIGHT 2000 BY JOANNE AMORT

ALL RIGHTS RESERVED. NO PART OF THIS BOOK MAY BE REPRODUCED IN ANY FORM OR BY ANY ELECTRONIC OR MECHANICAL MEANS, INCLUDING INFORMATION STORAGE AND RETRIEVAL SYSTEMS, WITHOUT THE PERMISSION IN WRITING FROM THE PUBLISHER, EXCEPT BY A REVIEWER WHO MAY QUOTE BRIEF PASSAGES IN A REVIEW.

FIRST EDITION: 5000 copies

Library of Congress Card Number: 00-108085

ISBN: 0-9704106-0-3

Designed by MICHAEL LEDET ART & DESIGN, New Orleans

Edited by Mimi Byrnes Pelton, New Orleans
Typography and production by Martin/Greater Communications, New Orleans

Published by Oak Alley Foundation, Vacherie, Louisiana

Cover Illustration: Courtesy of the Historic New Orleans Collection, Acc. No. 1982.96

PRINTED IN CANADA

To N.S.A.
Whose love forged all
my memories in gold

BEFORE WE BEGIN

*P*robing the past for the purpose of examining it in the light of the present can be tricky in that one is faced with the dilemma of interpretation. This is a problem without solution for the simple reason that recorded history is by nature the ultimate acceptance of a single point of view. To be sure, this acceptance is based on studies of endless documents, stories and traditions, but, in the end, there will never be more than one side of the coin showing. In any case, it is more than likely that the flip side will have become too faded to bother with anyway, and we will have to make do with what the most learned amongst us have decreed to be "the way it was".

Therefore, in preparing the following pages about a unique, short-lived moment in the history of this awesome River Region, logical conclusions, imagination and even a bit of the old cliché, "the proof's in the puddin", are pretty much the extent of my personal research. If the reader can feel enlightened, rewarded, entertained or simply relieved as the last page is turned, the blame or laurels shall rightly be placed on the shoulders of those who encouraged the whole project in the first place, and upon the true scholars who poured many combined years of research and love into the rich sources of information I relied upon so heavily.

I was challenged to tell this story, you see, by those who either thought I wouldn't, or felt I couldn't, or perhaps only wanted to keep me busy and out of trouble. Bless them all! To Ernest Posey and Zeb Mayhew, Jr., who were the challengers; to my children for their support and discernment; to Father Norman J. Rogge, S.J. for sharing with this old friend precious time, volumes of great personal research, and invaluable assistance in keeping the events in correct chronological order; to Mr. Julius Arceneaux for sharing thoughts drawn from his endeavors to validate aspects of his family's role in the colorful history of the river parishes; to the extraordinary research efforts of Vaughn Glasgow and Carol Hestor, who we pray will be inspired to complete *Kiss The Children For Me,* that long awaited, distinctive literary work about the Roman Family; to Stacy Atkins, Donna Amedee, and other kind souls who read over my efforts and, having done so, still encouraged me; to Mimi Byrnes Pelton, my expert and gentle editor, who, with Michael Ledet, master of art and design, took the freshly hatched "ugly duckling" manuscript under their wings and brought forth a graceful swan. For what it's worth, there would be nothing but blank pages and a very frustrated would-be author without each and every one of them ... my appreciation is boundless!

One last thought. Some of the characters are real people, and the incidents surrounding them and their lives, where documentation exists, did indeed take place. Still, woven into the fabric of accepted fact, are some flights of fancy and a roster of fictitious persons who, nevertheless, *could* have been as real as those extraordinary Creole giants of history with whom they are made to interact. However, the point here is, that rather than attempt to paint a literary portrait of well known personalities, this story's intent is merely to glimpse into events, customs and bits and pieces of plantation life along the Mississippi during an era aptly identified in Louisiana's history as The Golden Age.

So, I invite you now to sit back, imagine the sights, the sounds and sensations of 19th century River Road magic, and interpret it all as you will ...

Joanne Amort

J.T. Roman/Valcour Aime
Immediate Descendants

Jacques Telesphore Roman
1800-1848

Therese Celina Pilie
1816-1866

m. June, 1834

Louise (1835-1895)
Albert (1836-1838)
Marie Octavie (1837-1866)
George (1838-died in infancy)
Henri (1839-1905)
Marie (1840-1857)

*

*

François Gabriel "Valcour" Aime
1797-1867

Josephine Roman
1797-1856

m. January, 1819

Edwige (1820-1861)
Josephine (1821-1898)
Felicité Emma (1823-1905)
Felicie (1825-1857)
François Gabriel "Gabi" (1826-1854)

*Courtesy of the Historic New Orleans Collection, Detail, Acc. Nos. 1983.161.1 and 1983.161.2

.... there cannot be
growth without sacrifice,
and there is no guarantee
that what will come
tomorrow will be half as
precious as what was ours
just yesterday.

Jim Metcalf

From his Journal

Courtesy of the Historic New Orleans Collection, Acc. No. 1984.58.33

Oak Alley Plantation

CHAPTER I

The first time I saw that amazing alley of oak trees framing the stately, shell pink manor was in June of 1839. My parents and I were enjoying a fortnight at Le Petit Versailles in St. James Parish as house guests of the Valcour Aime family. Plans for the afternoon that day included a ride upriver to see what fresh additions had been made to J. T. Roman's proud new home, the groundbreaking of which had taken place two years before. The house itself, I later learned, had been declared complete only days before our visit and the adults in our group were particularly anxious to see the results. We were told that most of the remaining tasks now revolved around landscaping the spacious grounds and putting finishing touches to the neatly arranged outbuildings and kitchen.

Of course, none of us children felt that anything could possibly compare to the enchantment of Valcour Aime's famous Petit Versailles, with its 20 acres of gardens ablaze with exotic flowers and shrubs, a park that housed strange birds and animals (including a kangaroo), bridges over tiny streams, as well as a Chinese pagoda with tinkling bells. There was even a miniature fort complete with canon, spyglass and other marvels to trigger our imaginations and, if that were not enough, a little train which chugged merrily on rails throughout the plantation grounds. Assorted future projects were taking shape on the drafting table, and each time we visited we were astounded by the latest wonders being created before our eyes.

It was reasonable to assume that pulling us away from this veritable Shangri-la was not likely to be an easy task, but an outing on River Road suggested exciting possibilities as well and we offered surprisingly little resistance to being bundled into one of the larger carriages waiting in the drive. Off we went for the short ride up River Road; sounds of river traffic and the glimpse of an occasional smoke stack on our right, neatly manicured gardens and plantation homes on our left. There were enough of us youngsters to be annoyingly noisy, and our ever-present nannies were obliged to 'shush' us more than once so that the adults could 'hear themselves think'.

Totally adverse to being included in our rambunctious group was Emma Aime, already a young lady at 16. She was resigned to sit as far removed as she could from her 14 year old sister, Felicie, and their younger brother, Gabi, and me, since we were still mischievous and high-spirited, he having just turned 13 and I a year younger. The two Fortiers, Noel and Amy, first cousins to the Aimes, were also visiting the plantation. They were close in age to the three of us, and fit nicely enough in our midst, though an occasional dispute would arise about who was to be leader, or when the boys' logic of male superiority faced female challenges. It never lasted long, though, and we had always considered ourselves the best of friends.

We were engrossed in tentative plans for tomorrow's picnic on the levee, and the joys of inventing hair-raising adventure stories about sinister destinations of passing boats and their ill-fated passengers when, quite without warning, the clip-clopping of the horses stilled and we were there. Such a magical sight it was that every carriage passenger fell silent in awe. What lay before us was sheer beauty. The early afternoon sun dappled the green of the avenue and lent a glow to the house shimmering for all the world like mother of pearl. The coachmen were ordered to pause for several moments as we absorbed the essence of "Telesphore Roman's Place." "Well done, Telesphore," we heard M. Aime murmur as the caravan proceeded on up the tree covered approach to where the Romans waited to receive us.

Once we had properly greeted our hosts with our polished bows and curtseys, we were free to romp in the cool of the great oaks. The Romans had two daughters and a two month old baby boy, Henri. Louise, the eldest, was four and Marie Octavie had just turned two. For the most part, we considered even the girls too small to take part in our activities, but they turned out to be well behaved and generously brought out all manner of toys and games for our entertainment. The adults settled in on the verandah where an elegant tea and iced drinks laced with fragrant flower petals had been served. We found that our own table had been set up under one of the trees. There were delightful little cakes with orange blossoms encrusted in icing, fresh slices of bread with creamy butter and blackberry jam, tiny tarts still warm from the oven and, of course, our tea with cream and sugar. We ate with the enthusiasm of healthy young creatures and soon headed back to continue our play. We eagerly accepted Louise's invitation to see the herb gardens set near the new kitchen still under construction, and the *pigeonniers,* filled with fat and glistening birds, set at each side of the rear entrance of the home. A peacock the color of jewels fanned his tail in flirtatious display before a rather nondescript mate, prompting Gabi's snide remark about how naturally drab females were. He insisted, running away as we pelted him with dirt clods, that he was talking about birds, not people, but the fuss was forgotten by the time we reached the back of the house.

The vast acreage spread out before us was filled with all the basics required for smooth operation of a large plantation. There were several varieties of domestic animals and fowl, and a huge stable housed a number of M. Roman's prized thoroughbreds. An enthusiastic horseman and hunter, M. Roman had a most impressive array of fine gear arranged in a special loft room.

Over 20 neat slave cabins lined the roads leading to the cane fields and fruit orchards to the south, and a fine new sugar house split the road into two wide paths at the far end. The orchards boasted pecans, oranges, lemons, plums and fig trees, many laden with ripening fruit. Growing along the sides of buildings were juicy raspberries, blackberries and blueberries practically screaming to be picked and gobbled up by enthusiastic youngsters! Louise followed us around the spacious grounds, pointing proudly to a number of things that testified to the magnitude of the plantation, and to her family's social status. Since we were all related in one way or another, her childish boasting was in no way offensive, and we readily agreed that we were undoubtedly an extraordinary bunch.

By the time we returned to the front verandah the afternoon was far spent, and the carriages ready and waiting for the trip back to Le Petit Versailles. It had been a most memorable first visit to Oak Alley Plantation, and we kept looking back and waving until the lovely home faded from view when we turned onto River Road.

That night my mother told me more about the Roman family. Mother and Tante Jo had been dear friends since infancy and were related through the D'Aigles, who had immigrated from Canada in the mid 1700's. She spoke of the fun they had growing up together; of summers spent on family plantations, the excitement of the social season in the

Vieux Carre, and of Tante Jo's many handsome brothers, including Governor André Bienvenu, and the youngest, Jacques Telesphore, who had been our gracious host that day.

Mother said that she could never remember a time when Tante Jo and Valcour Aime had not been in love with each other. She explained to me that Oncle Valcour's real name was François Gabriel, and that he and his brother, Michel, had been orphaned at a tender age. They grew up in the care of their grandfather, Michel Fortier II, and it had been their beloved nanny who had affectionately called the younger of her two wards Valcour, a name he treasured and preferred as his signature.

Mother's description of the devoted couple was so romantic. She told me about their long and steady courtship and what a handsome figure he had cut when, at the age of 16, Valcour and his older brother, Michel, saw action in The Battle of New Orleans. My father had also served in this battle, as did all the Roman brothers – Jacques, the youngest, was only 14 and Mother and Tante Jo dreamily shared their pride and concern for the safety of their beaux/heros. Seven years later, Valcour Aime and Josephine Roman were married. The marriage contract was signed in January of 1819 at the Roman family estate in St. James Parish, followed within a week by the celebration of a most elegant and solemn church wedding at St. Louis Cathedral in New Orleans.

Tante Jo's father, Jacques Etienne Roman, had died a few years before, leaving a sizable fortune to be divided amongst his widow and surviving children. As a result, Tante Jo brought to her marriage a substantial dowry, plus the use of her mother's St. James Parish plantation home. So it was there that the newlyweds chose to take up permanent residence, in that fertile and now flourishing River Parish. Proceeds from the sale of Valcour's St. Charles Parish properties to his brother, Michel, brought the combined fortunes of the happy couple to new and impressive heights. It also assured the realization of many of their dreams for renovating the existing plantation house and extensive grounds, a venture set in motion almost immediately.

What exciting images Mother's words painted for me! Parties, receptions, and all kinds of celebrations seemed to fill almost every moment of the social calendar in the city and throughout the River Parishes. Mother and my father, also childhood sweethearts, were married shortly after the Aimes, in March of 1819. Although my parents intended to live in the city and the Aimes had moved to the country, the two couples were delighted to find that neither distance nor changes in priorities common to married life had weakened their deep friendship in any way. In fact, they now found themselves sharing even more memorable occasions together as they crossed over the threshold into a Golden Age.

The next day dawned crisp and clear, perfect for the

realization of the plans we had made during the carriage ride to Oak Alley. We ran to find Simon, who had agreed to supervise preparations for our picnic. Simon was the Aime's devoted butler, and although he had received his freedom last January 6th as a Christmas gift, he unhesitatingly chose to remain with his beloved master in a salaried capacity. As a freedman, Simon could purchase the freedom of his wife, Sarah, and his little family then joined others whom Valcour Aime had liberated but who would not leave him and the security of the only true home they had known. Of Simon and Sarah's children, two young sons, Matthew and Marc, had always been playmates for Gabi, and it was these brothers their father sent to the selected picnic spot to arrange the blankets and basket of goodies under one of the many willow trees lining the river side of the levee.

By 11:00 o'clock we could no longer be contained and were given permission to set out toward the levee where we could see the two boys busy with preparations. Ah youth! Oh, unsuspecting parenthood! The innocent smiles on the faces of Tante Jo, Mother *and* Simon were radiant as each imagined the angelic pursuits of their dear children. As for us, leaving our nannies far behind, we ran like wild things down the tree lined path from the Big House, across River Road and up the green embankment where exotic worlds, heros and heroines, fierce monsters and fairy godmothers awaited us.

More than that awaited us, we soon discovered! A

large green lizard, tucked in the picnic basket by a gleeful Matt and Marc, leaped into my lap and set the girls to shrieking hysterically while Gabi and Noel felt duty bound to chase the delighted perpetrators with threats of revenge. They were soon back to flop down panting from the exertion. Even though we were all playmates and never tattled on each other, Gabi suggested he just might drop a hint to Simon about the lizard. Everyone knew he wouldn't, though, partly because Matt and Marc were well-armed with details of Gabi's own history of adolescent mischief.

It was a cloudless day, too early in the summer to be hot and humid, with a north breeze blowing gently across the river. From our vantage point we could see from bend to bend in the Mississippi, as well as all kinds of activity taking place on the opposite bank. Of course, what we couldn't actually see, we imagined, and it was here that the real fun began to unfold.

Brightly colored paddle-wheelers, some bearing elegantly clad passengers, filled the air with clanging bells and loud puffing of tall smoke stacks. Others, smaller and full of cargo, plied the river, either heading upriver or returning to New Orleans. There were barges, steamers in assorted sizes, and even an occasional keelboat, while each wharf, large or small, within the scope of our vision, seemed bustling with purpose. At a short distance upriver, we could see the pier stretching into the water in front of Le Petit Versailles. It, too, was the center of loading and unloading

Courtesy of the Historic New Orleans Collection, Detail, Acc. No. 1974.25.30.728

Steamboating on the Mississippi River

one of the steamer packets which regularly spanned the watery distance between the big cities and the plantations.

The one we saw today was the *Robert Fulton*. After unloading all manner of tools, luxury goods and mail, she was to pick up, in return, assorted outgoing farm products and correspondence. Gabi proudly described the riverboat his father had commissioned to be built for the family's personal use and which would be christened the *Gabriel Aime*. She was to be the very top of the line in every way and appointed with the finest in luxury accommodations. Additionally, she would be equipped to handle practical cargoes as required for plantation operation and growth. On that very day, Gabi generously invited us all to be there for the christening. It wasn't too clear when that might be, but we were invited anyway.

Amy gingerly opened the picnic basket to see if there were any refreshments left. She dropped the lid once with a squeak when one of the boys jumped at her, but then realized the supply of lizards had run out and that there were enough snacks to go around one more time. We picked up where we'd left off with outlandish tales of maritime horrors assigned to each passing vessel. Even Oncle Valcour's prized kangaroo became a topic of our fancies when Gabi described the day the 'roo arrived in a giant cage.

The kangaroo was, our story teller explained, a gift from a retired English sea captain who had lived in New South Wales during the short but colorful governorship of part hero/part fiend William "Bounty" Bligh, and had amused himself collecting specimens of the strange animals and plant life which are said to abound in that exotic land. Naturally, our captain friend was gruesomely possessed of a peg leg, a hook for his left hand, a hideously scarred face and no teeth, but the story unfolded smoothly to our wide-eyed delight. Noel, secretly doubting much of Gabi's version of how the 'roo made it to Louisiana's shores, wanted to know why there wasn't a pair of them and was assured that there had, indeed, been a mate, but that she had lept overboard in sorrow at being taken from her homeland. Only Old 'Roo survived the journey and took up life, serenely content, in the lush gardens of Le Petit Versailles.

Some serious ghosts bent on revenge for murderous deeds and unrequited love also evolved from our wild imaginations that afternoon, and we scarcely noticed the sun sinking lower on the horizon. Soon the sound of the plantation bell calling the field hands in reminded us that it was time to head home. Matt and Marc began picking up the blankets and remains of our picnic. The nannies, who at this point in our lives we regarded as totally unnecessary, had been dozing peacefully in the shade of a tree and had to be awakened . This was accomplished amid embarrassed assurances that they had *not* been sleeping, had heard every word, and had their eyes closed because of the bright sun. Well, one of them had been snoring, but it didn't matter because we seldom tattled on our nannies either. We tolerated their presence quietly enough, and had learned early on that laxness on their part usually translated into more freedom for us.

Reluctantly, we turned away from the river and started down the levee, amazed at how quickly the day had faded into evening. Another moment with good friends and family had become a memory.

After dinner I reminded Mother of her promise to continue with the story of the Romans, the Aimes, and us. For once, she had no trouble getting me to prepare for bed and found me waiting eagerly for her to pick up the thread of her narrative. She agreed that it was a very romantic story, but reminded me that joy would always be laced with sadness, profit with loss, and days of plenty with times of deprivation. It was then that she told me about the first two babies she had lost. One little son had died within an hour of his birth. Then there was the terrible disappointment of the miscarriage of a second child not long after that. She and my father had been broken hearted, especially with the bitter sweet news of the arrival first of little Edwige Aime in 1820, then Josephine in 1821, followed in rapid succession by Emma (full name Felicité Emma) in 1823, and Felicie in late 1825. Although my parents were truly happy for the blessings showered on their dear friends, the cloud of the loss of their own little ones hung over their joy. Of course, my arrival in November of 1827 was cause for celebration, I was assured, and helped heal the emptiness. Gabriel, "Gabi", the Aime's long awaited son, had joined the family a year before, and the future glowed with promise for good things yet to come.

Mother paused for a moment to gather her thoughts. I tugged impatiently at her sleeve and begged her to go on with the story. She patted my arm, smiled in recollection, and resumed her account of what followed.

In October of 1830, Tante Jo's mother died in the family townhouse on Rue Dumaine. Six years later, when her succession was probated, her youngest son, Jacques Telesphore, bought from the estate the old Roman family homestead where Oncle Valcour and Tante Jo were presently living. As soon as that transaction was signed and sealed, M. Roman sold the same property to his brother-in-law. Valcour Aime, in turn, sold J. T. Roman a plot of adjoining land acquired shortly after his marriage to Tante Jo.

It was this land that interested Telesphore as a perfect site to build what was to become his Oak Alley Plantation home. Obviously, the presence of the avenue of huge oak trees was what distinguished this particular river front acreage from others, in that the trees had already attained significant size and maturity when the Aimes bought it in 1820. There are members of the Arceneaux family who believe that their ancestor, Michel, acquired this same plot of land nearly a century ago, and planted 40 identifying oak trees leading from the river's edge to his hunting lodge. If so, either the Mississippi River or man's quest for more dwelling space must have made off with twelve of the trees, but it was still exciting for me to imagine that the cool alley of oaks that we children had happily romped in yesterday had perhaps been there for a hundred years.

In May of 1836, the two brothers-in-law, by exchanging properties and other assets, acquired total ownership of their respective plantations and could now give full vent to their dreams of creating estates that would be known far and wide for their grandeur, their productivity, and exceptional beauty.

We spent two unforgettable weeks at Le Petit Versailles during that particular June visit to the River Parishes, and enjoyed several other afternoons with the Roman family. We watched with genuine interest as work continued at both plantations. At Le Petit Versailles, Oncle Valcour had been constantly adding on to the original house, as well as building up his already remarkable "English Gardens". As viewed from the levee, the façades of the two houses actually resembled one another, with huge pillars and deep galleries, although the floor plans differed considerably, that of the Aime's manor having a U-shape. Both were considered fine examples of the quite popular Greek Revival type of architecture. Celina Roman had attempted to rename their plantation Bon Sejour, but neighbors and riverboat captains would forever refer to it as Oak Alley or Telesphore Roman's place.

During one of our visits, we positioned ourselves on a lower limb of one of the alley oaks to observe as the new garçonnieres flanking the front entrance gardens were being painted. The same pale pink as the house had been chosen for the whitewash color, and Gabi and I later managed to get into a bit of trouble by making our own mixture of lime, whey and red clay and splashing each other with the corn husk brushes the busy slaves were using for painting. Not a good idea! We were scolded and sent to find something to do which would be less threatening to our clothes.

Courtesy of the Historic New Orleans Collection, Detail, Acc. No. 1974.25.30.722

Hailing the Steamboat

CHAPTER II

*S*hortly after the announcement of Emma's engagement to Alex Fortier in January of 1841, we all gathered once again at Le Petit Versailles for a wonderful riverside celebration marking the christening of the long awaited steamboat *Gabriel Aime*. As he'd promised us during that picnic 18 months before, Gabi formally invited me, Amy and Noel to join him dockside for the big moment. And what a moment it was! Before us, in gleaming splendor, was a beautiful vessel, quite the most spectacular on the river. Although not as large as some of the commercial steamboats, it was fit for a king in every way. Father A. P. Ladaviere, Pastor at St. James Church, had arrived the evening before so he could be present the next morning to celebrate a special Mass in the great hall of the Big House. He was also to officiate at the blessing scheduled to precede Valcour Aime's novel idea of a champagne-laced christening later in the afternoon. The *Gabriel Aime* was festooned with streamers, her brass fixtures shone, her windows sparkled, and crystal chandeliers glistened through the open doors of the elegant salon deck. Our curiosity was aroused by what looked like a hedge of potted flowering shrubs enclosing a top deck aft area. Gabi grinned at our questions and told us to prepare for a big surprise as soon as the champagne bottle broke over her bow, but adamantly refused to reveal more.

The Aime's slave, André, a talented chef, had quite outdone himself for the occasion. The succulent feast set up under striped tents was evidence of his epicurean skills. André was the reason for a great deal of envy experienced by all who had been fortunate enough to dine with the Aimes. Many a distinguished member of New Orleans society had offered Valcour enormous amounts of money for him, but Valcour would have none of it. Indeed, having seen to André's apprenticeship in Paris under the best chefs, he then appointed André to head the entire kitchen domain, and soon there were a number of assistants training under André's watchful eye. It had often been observed that there were few tables set in the country that even approached the degree of culinary perfection served daily at Le Petit Versailles.

Beyond doubt, the whole scene was no less than a lavish wonderland. Ladies in afternoon gowns, colorful bonnets, parasols and shawls, formed groups with gentlemen in frock coats and top hats to partake of the feast, the free flowing wine and to enjoy the music provided by a string quartet located under a tent near the pier. I was delighted to see Amy and Noel and hear what had been going on in their lives, and it wasn't long before I realized that my parents had moved toward an arrangement of canopied benches so that Mother, who was expecting a child in late June, could rest. Climbing on a big rock near the gangplank, I spotted what looked like Mother's plumed bonnet and began to wind my way toward them. Louise Roman saw me go by and ran over to say hello and to pull me by the hand to the spot where her parents were seated on lawn chairs in the shade of a willow tree. I curtseyed properly, congratulated them on the recent arrival of little Marie and asked how she was doing.

News from Oak Alley appeared to be good, and Celina, whose somewhat delicate last confinement had obliged her to postpone her usual September return to New Orleans, seemed especially overjoyed at this opportunity to mingle with so many friends on hand from the city. Even I could provide her with bits and pieces of gossip I'd overheard about this person or that, and her many questions and obvious interest made me feel quite important and grown up. Indeed, we were all having a great time visiting with old friends, meeting new ones, and, in general, enjoying a matchless day of swift moving hours and splendid entertainment. How nice it was!

In addition to the long guest list of important family members and friends in attendance, all 200 of Valcour

Aime's plantation slaves, not to mention freedmen and a few highly specialized employees, were there. Needless to say, the large downriver section of the levee arranged for them was already alive with excitement and good food, while sounds of fiddles and banjos could be heard preparing for a more carefree display of fun. It was easy to see why the levee was literally filled with people from one bend in the river to the other. No matter which direction one walked in there was merriment to be found.

At 3:00 o'clock sharp, we were approached by white jacketed servants who informed us that the ceremony was about to begin. It seemed that even the river traffic quieted down for the blessing. Then Valcour took Tante Jo by the arm and led her to the end of the pier where she was handed a bottle of champagne tied with white satin ribbons. She looked at it questioningly, but smiled with delight as her husband whispered something in her ear. Then, with her hand on his for support, she stepped forward, said the words, "I name thee *Gabriel Aime*", and broke the bottle with one stroke . As the champagne splashed on the bow, spraying all who were near, fireworks began to explode up and down the levee, steamboat whistles blew and, suddenly, the surprise Gabi had promised made itself known to all. Included in the *Gabriel Aime's* luxuries, and unbeknownst to even Tante Jo, was a fine calliope. It was what the potted plants we'd already wondered about had concealed. During the blessing and christening the captain had ordered that steam be built up so that the calliope could pipe out some of the latest songs. What a spectacle! Passing riverboats signaled us, their passengers and crew waving excitedly, and both banks of the river exploded in boisterous display as all joined in celebrating the joyful event.

With the momentum of the down river revelers' festivities in full swing, it was now time for the rest of us to file on board for a closer inspection of the awe-inspiring vessel. The Aime family arranged themselves on deck by the gangplank to receive their guests. More refreshments were served in the dining room and on the upper deck, while folks gathered around the calliope to request different tunes from the happy man at the keyboard who would play as long as the steam held out. The quartet had also come on board and continued to provide music in the salon. Truly an unforgettable occasion, the shipboard party continued until night had fallen and the stars became a formidable backdrop for the waning hours of celebration.

So began the luxurious *Gabriel Aime's* long and colorful career on the Mississippi. There would be many shipboard parties hosted on her polished decks, and she was destined to play an important role in the family's joys and many sorrows from that day forward.

The Sugar Mill.

J. Durkin
87.

Courtesy of the Historic New Orleans Collection, Detail, Acc. No. 1975.46

Harvesting the Sugar Cane

CHAPTER III

*L*ate fall of 1843 was memorable for me in particular. To mark the end of a profitable cane cutting season, a huge party was being staged at Oak Alley and we were all to attend the day-long festivities. Gabi, then tall and handsome at 17, had invited school mates from nearby Jefferson College to spend a week or so at Le Petit Versailles, and a long stretch of River Road literally bristled with anticipation and excitement.

The day dawned clear and warm. Not long before midday, my family and I joined other arrivals in the inspiring drive up the beautiful alley of oak trees. We could hear music from somewhere on the lush grounds and the mouth watering smells of roasting meats and simmering gumbo pots filled the air. Our hosts were receiving their guests about half way up the alley where a colorful tent had been set up. I was truly shocked to see how frail M. Roman seemed. Many guests noticed that he was obliged to withdraw from the receiving line every so often to rest in a chair placed nearby. I nudged Mother questioningly and she said the family had been concerned about his health for some time, but that Madame Roman had brushed the whole thing off by suggesting that it was something her husband had trumped up to avoid attending social affairs in New Orleans during the current opera season. It occurred to me that I would ask Louise about her father as soon as I could catch her alone. Although she was not quite nine, she had always been a bright child and responsible beyond her years. I felt sure she would be well informed of the true situation.

It was impossible not to notice Gabi standing on the terrace with several young men. A bevy of girls giggling in blushing admiration were nearby. As I passed them on my way toward the open doors of the house in search of some of my school friends, Gabi sprang forward and gave me an enthusiastic hug. We had hardly seen each other since Emma's marriage to Alex Fortier two years before, and were surprised to note that between school, Gabi's trips to Europe, and my own preoccupation with becoming a young lady, time had pretty much flown by. Gabi presented two of his friends, and my original path toward the drawing room developed a decided fork in the road. Suddenly, it was much more interesting right where I was. Gabi's 18 year old friend, Tony, instantly made a good impression on me. The son of a prominent businessman from Donaldsonville,

Tony was in his last year at Jefferson College, and had known Gabi for several years. He was a great conversationalist, was witty, and had sparkling blue eyes. The other young man, Charles, was from New Orleans, and was also a student at the college. At this juncture I found myself torn between two very interesting gentlemen. Could I dare to hope that *both* of them would pay attention to me? Perhaps even invite me to have barbecue with them? Since neither of them excused himself and walked away, I decided there were interesting possibilities still ahead that fine day.

I was troubled, though. Things seemed to have changed between Gabi and me. We weren't as relaxed with one another and I found myself suddenly self-conscious. What a shame, I thought. Our wonderful childhood friendship was now strained as I saw him grown to manhood and he viewed me as a "member of the gentler sex". I could see it in his eyes and it made me sad. He had become enormously popular and his latest interests focused on developing social graces and flattering banter with the ladies, something in which he clearly excelled. I turned again to Tony and Charles. As I'd hoped, they invited me to sit with them at the barbecue, and my dance card was almost entirely filled with their names. It did appear that both of them liked me and I considered for a brief moment the flattering possibility of *two* suitors. Such a scenario had never occurred to me before because, though there were those who said I was pretty, I had never really dared to take such comments seriously.

In any case, my romantic dream triangle was soon shattered when Gabi made mention of Tony's determination to enter the priesthood after his graduation. So much for *that!* Still, Charles continued to circle the arena with some show of determination, and asked if he might call on me at home once we'd returned to New Orleans. Of course, I assured him that it would be a pleasure to receive his visit, and inwardly hoped that my enthusiasm wasn't too evident.

Following the barbecue, most of the gentlemen withdrew to the parlor for the customary tobacco and brandy. This was a much anticipated respite in which the latest news from the world of business, politics, and local gossip was to be shared. The ladies, meanwhile, retired to rest in anticipation of the late afternoon ribbon ceremony, and the dance that night. From the balcony one could see luminaries lining either side of the avenue of great oaks, and the immaculately trimmed lawn already beckoned to those who might later be anxious to show off some of the latest reels. Quite naturally, there were few, if any, young girls who did much resting that day, as whispers, giggles and shared secrets took top priority.

I found Louise in the upstairs hallway and was finally able to ask after her father. She told me that he had been suffering from gout and painful arthritis which were causing him no little discomfort. She also shared their doctor's opinion that M. Roman was showing decided symptoms of tuberculosis and, as Mother had already told me, the family was quite concerned. Of course, Louise's innate loyalty to her parents precluded my probing deeper into the matter of Madame Roman's mocking remarks about what she called her husband's senseless distaste for city life and preference for his boring plantation. Louise, young as she was, must have been well aware of her mother's grievances because the comments had been frequent and quite public, and had already kindled the flames of local gossip. Mother had witnessed Celina's railing at a recent afternoon tea, and was both shocked and deeply troubled at the vindictiveness and total injustice of the accusations. Such a sad situation! I could not help but think it callous of Madame Roman to not only ignore her gentle husband's obvious poor health, but also to attribute it to something as silly as lack of enthusiasm for the New Orleans opera season!

Just before three in the afternoon, the sound of music and excited voices signaling the official end of the harvest could be heard through the open bedroom windows. Everyone was up and about in a flash, followed by a mad rush to prepare for the festivities. A veritable cascade of brightly clad ladies soon filled the staircase, their wide hoops, parasols and broad-brimmed hats obliging them to descend in single file. I decided to wait until the crowd had thinned out somewhat and went out onto the balcony.

From the southwest corner I could see across the cane

fields where the slaves had gathered to await the ceremonial cutting of the last stalk. There were a number of gaily decorated wagons standing by for the parade around the plantation grounds, and guests from the Big House were already starting to pour out of doors on their way toward the merriment. After a quick look in one of the mirrors to make sure I had everything in place, I grabbed my shawl and joined the throng heading toward the fields.

Half way down the back walkway I found Charles leaning against one of the oaks, a grin on his face and a red rose in his hand. He stepped forward, handed me the rose and asked if he could walk with me. We let most of the people go by and slowed our pace so that we could talk together. It was so nice having him at my side and I hoped he had intentions of spending a great deal of the rest of the evening's activities with me.

By the time we reached the fields, the ceremonial last stalk had just been cut amid shouts of joy. The stalk, adorned with a big straw hat, was then tied with bright ribbons, was lifted high in the air and waved for all to see, as it was carried onto the wagon standing first in line. All hands scrambled into as many other wagons as would hold them and the parade began. We followed part of the way and then turned back to the house where signs and sounds of the dinner and dancing yet to come were all around. A group of our friends had assembled on the balcony to watch the festivities, and we joined them to share comments about the gaiety unfolding before us.

Meanwhile, the wagons filled with celebrating workers continued their trek around the grounds. The parade's ultimate destination was a picnic area where feasting and games would take place until the wee hours. A happy bunch indeed, with the long shifts and hard work over at last, they were more than ready to celebrate, and looked forward eagerly to the promised week long holiday which lay ahead. Fiddles, tambourines, and the twang of banjos set a pace that was contagious and kept even the most demure foot tapping. There was no doubt in our minds that the music and dancing from that already rollicking sector of the plantation would unfold in a whirl of calico, bright petticoats and flashing eyes. What a sight it would be! Many of the younger set intended to wander down later to join in the excitement, and they would not be disappointed.

Admittedly, this had not been the first time I'd witnessed the last stalk ceremony. Partly out of concern for my little brother, whose infancy had been stressed by bouts of childhood illnesses, but mostly because it was such fun, the family had made it routine to move out of the city to the country during both the sultry heat of summer and again toward the end of the year. We loved these visits, especially the ones which coincided with grinding season at the sugar plantations. To this day, the very thought of dipping strings of pecans in kettles of boiling cane syrup and savoring that unique praline flavor makes my mouth water! Yes, there were always exciting things going on in the country; harvesting took place each year, and the better the crop, the greater the celebration. Even so, this one in the year 1843 was made unique for me by the presence of a certain young man named Charles. It was he, whose warm smile and gentle ways, etched forever in gold my impression of that late summer evening at Oak Alley.

CHAPTER IV

We had been back home for only a few days when Charles came to call. He had a few more days before returning to Jefferson College and appeared intent on spending as much time as was seemly in courting me. Fortunately, our home was in the 600 block of Rue Dauphine and Charles' family lived not far away on Rue St. Ann. Our parents seemed genuinely pleased about it all and there were no obstacles to overcome from that very important sector. By the time Charles' vacation was over, we were considered a couple and were included as such in social activities. Autumn had swiftly faded into frosty mornings, and I, for one, had never been happier.

The day Charles returned to college, his family invited me to join them dockside to see him off. Though I tried not to be emotional, the minute the big red paddlewheel started to turn I had to fight the tears, while the boat carrying that special person on the upper deck grew smaller and smaller, and finally disappeared around the crescent-shaped bend of the river.

School terms in those days spanned almost the entire year, with only short breaks now and then, a week or so in fall, and time off for the sacred holidays of Christmas and Easter. It would seem like an eternity before Charles would be back and we could see each other again. And yet, the sudden hope that Mother might be persuaded to visit Tante Jo gave me something to think about. Then, too, Gabi might just consider inviting a certain school friend to spend a weekend with him at Petit Versailles. Hmmmmm! I smiled contentedly at Charles' mother, father and sister, and headed back with them to the waiting carriage.

Letters began to flow between us. He wrote faithfully twice a week and I answered each one by the very next mail packet. As it turned out, the Aimes, accompanied by the usual large retinue of servants, came to the city in mid November to attend a number of social and business engagements. Of course, it was nice to see them, but their agenda definitely did not allow for any hope of the realization of my somewhat devious plans to see Charles at Le Petit Versailles. Besides, the weeks were flying by and soon Charles would be home for the holidays. We had become, in no uncertain terms, devoted to each other, and so we would remain. Thinking of different ways to please one another took on new significance, and where occasional selfishness had been part of my own pampered childhood, family members began to remark on a number of unusual signs of thoughtfulness, and mistakenly attributed it entirely to impending maturity.

Sentimentality and romantic gestures were not limited to young lovers, I learned, when Mother shared with us the details of Oncle Valcour's latest show of devotion to Tante Jo. This amazing venture originated during that same November visit to the city. It began following a luncheon at the St. Charles Avenue home of a prominent businessman who, despite the fact that he was an American, had become a good friend of the Aime family. On their way back toward the Vieux Carré, M. Aime asked the carriage driver to let them off on Prytania Street so they could stroll through the much touted Garden District and see some of the elegant new homes lining both sides of the boulevard. Tante Jo paused at one address to admire a pair of magnificent trees, the branches of which shaded the lovely garden, the sidewalk and even most of the street. She remarked that she had seen none in all of St. James Parish to compare with them, not even the oaks at her brother's famous Oak Alley. "Would they not look superb in front of our house?", she asked her husband. He nodded with a smile, then hailed the carriage which had been following at a discreet distance, suggesting that it was now time for them to return to the hotel to prepare for dinner.

The next day he was gone for a few hours 'on business'. At lunch he told his wife that she might wish to make additional plans for a bit more Christmas shopping

Courtesy of the Historic New Orleans Collection, Detail, Acc. No. 00.41

Southern Hospitality

and luncheon dates with friends because their return trip to Le Petit Versailles would have to be delayed and he didn't want her to be bored. Five days later they boarded the *Gabriel Aime* for the trip back. Tante Jo expressed surprise to find their personal vessel waiting at the dock because she had been led to understand that they were returning with friends from St. John Parish on the *Princess*. The delightfully imaginative Valcour quickly satisfied her curiosity by explaining that he wished to enjoy the return trip in the comfort of their own luxurious accommodations and, besides, that their friends had already left for home. The next morning when the boat docked and they stepped onto the levee in front of Le Petit Versailles, Tante Jo was astounded to see that the same two giant trees she had so admired on Prytania Street now graced the entrance to her plantation home.

Valcour had spared no expense in having the massive trees dug up, huge roots and all, and towed on barges by steamboat to St. James. The carefully blanketed roots and as much soil as would cling to them had to be kept moist, and the branches protected from breaking during the amazing transfer from city to country. Imagine the significance of this awesome undertaking! The owner of those trees had to be royally recompensed, and a small army of laborers hired to perform the task of uprooting the trees. They hauled each behemoth through city streets to the river, refilled the massive holes left in their stead, and then had to landscape the entire front garden from which they had been removed.

Meanwhile, at Le Petit Versailles, orders had been given to prepare two pits deep enough and wide enough to receive the gargantuan roots packed with soil from Prytania Street. All this had to be accomplished quickly before Tante Jo might become suspicious of her husband's activities and the surprise would be ruined. Tante Jo later told Mother she was so overwhelmed when she understood what had taken place that she nearly fainted. She said that Oncle Valcour was as excited as a little boy at Christmas time to see how delighted she was with his gift.

How typical of Valcour Aime! His greatest joy was in finding ways to please his wife. I made a mental note to describe to Charles in dramatic and somewhat pointed detail this knightly example of marital devotion. Not that Charles wasn't by nature a gentle and considerate person, but could any suitor, young or old, deny that there was much to learn from the likes of Valcour Aime? I wondered if it had occurred to Gabi that it was about time to move on from his flirtations, seek a special someone, and emulate the qualities of his father.

CHAPTER V

*T*ime continued its relentless passage through our lives. A little sister joined the family and instantly became the object of everyone's devotion. In December of 1845, Charles asked for my hand in marriage and on Christmas Eve presented me with a beautiful diamond and sapphire ring. Our engagement was formally announced at a reception held at home on the 15th of January, 1846. The wedding would take place in June of the following year, and planning for the event was already underway.

Felicie Aime and Amy Fortier would be two of my attendants, while cousins and one very close school friend completed the rest. My brother and Henri Roman were to be ring bearers. Charles had invited Gabi to be his best man, and Noel was among the ushers. Tony was now a seminarian in St. Louis, Missouri, and we would have to wait and see if he would be permitted to join us.

Arrangements had been made for the Nuptial Mass to take place at St. Louis Cathedral and the date was finally set for the 30th of June. So much to do! There were parties, shopping for a suitable trousseau and, of course, the seemingly endless fittings and detailing of the wedding gown. The many months were gone in a minute, and we began to measure time in weeks.

It seemed I had lost contact with just about everything outside the wedding preparations and only an occasional piece of news reached my ears about what might be going on in the River Parishes. Madame Roman and children had been in town for some time, but it was said that M. Roman was unable to travel and had preferred to remain at Oak Alley. Both Oncle Valcour and Tante Jo kept an eye on him and saw that those assigned to tend to him were diligent in their duties. Still, Tante Jo told Mother of her increasing concern for his failing health. Consumption, now undeniably present, was an illness which would run its course no matter what, and the eventual outcome was almost always dismal. There were some remedies, but M. Roman had tried them all. Rest and quiet was what he longed for and, so said the attending physician, would do him as much good as anything at this stage.

Tante Jo was somewhat relieved when, given the extent of her brother's increasingly restricted activities, Lottie, Oak Alley's rather imposing housekeeper and sovereign of the Big House staff and daily work agenda, had agreed that her youngest daughter, Celestine, be allowed to serve as courier between M. Roman and various work centers throughout the plantation. Celestine was a quiet and rather fragile child, very devoted to her ailing master, and happy to be the bearer of messages to and from whatever center of operations his vacillating physical condition confined him to each day.

Sometimes he would just sit in a chair on the balcony overlooking the alley of oaks and would read to Celestine. He was clearly pleased at how easily she recalled every detail as a story unfolded, and how she was able to associate letters with sounds, written words with spoken ones and whole sentences with the world around her. In short, Celestine was learning to read! Lottie snorted at any reference to these skills, arguing that such foolishness did no more than fill the child's mind with useless notions sure to make her neglect her duties. Louise told us later that, despite Lottie's contempt for learning, M. Roman had quite defied the rules by giving Celestine a book which the child kept hidden behind a loose board near her bed.

Louise, with her usual depth of perception, remarked several times that she believed her father's affection for little Celestine reflected how much he longed for the presence of his own children. She told Tante Jo that she would gladly have stayed with him all the time, but that her mother demanded that all her children accompany her in unending social affaires. It seemed clear to all of us that Celina would forever cling blindly to her conviction that Telesphore was only being selfish, and that it was she who should be pitied, not such a man who would deprive his devoted wife of regular contact with her beloved city. "Besides," she often said, "if indeed he is as ill as he claims, he is assured of better medical care in town than what some country bumpkin might pull out of his bag of tricks. No doubt about it. He is just being pigheaded!"

Meanwhile, letters to his family showed the "pigheaded" one to be experiencing fewer good days and ever increasing bad ones. Although he managed to maintain a sense of humor, M. Roman's usually precise handwriting often betrayed the acute distress of his afflictions. Such a patient and gentle man! We were all quite devoted to him, visited him when time and travel schedules allowed, and shared a genuine concern laced with frequent prayers for his well being. Both Charles and I deeply regretted that his poor health would not permit him to be present when we exchanged vows.

CHAPTER VI

*A*s our wedding day drew near, family members and friends began to assemble at the elegant St. Charles Hotel and in lodgings throughout the city. It was to be quite an affaire. I was excited, but was beginning to feel rather overwhelmed by all the forced activity. Charles and I hardly saw each other, although we had enjoyed a brief afternoon together spent strolling down shaded avenues lined by charming homes and lovely gardens. We playfully decided to add excitement to our walk by turning down streets where it was said were one or two haunted mansions.

We were particularly intrigued as we passed near the one where a riot in 1834 had broken out following reports of the infamous Madame Lalaurie's cruelty to her slaves. It was known that she narrowly escaped the city to France where, we were sure, she must still be cringing for her wickedness. Sadly, no ghosts showed up to enliven our walk, unless it was that strange looking being in a white cap who was furiously shaking so much dust from a mat that the entire spectacle resembled some sort of other-worldly scene. We both admitted to feeling sorry for the poor mat and wondered what it could possibly have done to merit such violent treatment. We were still laughing when we walked in the door at home and, when asked what we'd seen, could offer no plausible explanation for having spent the afternoon contemplating haunted houses.

That evening, Father announced with great pride that he and Charles' father had purchased a pretty little cottage for us on Rue Iberville. It was to be a surprise wedding present, but neither could contain his excitement in anticipation of our happiness with the wonderful gift. Indeed, parents on both sides were having such fun there wasn't much we could do but wait until we were married and assume that then we would be expected to lead our own lives. Meantime, an almost overwhelming display of good intentions on the part of family and close friends demanded that we show constant appreciation, so we did our best.

Charles had joined his father's firm shortly after graduation and had been made junior partner. He seemed to be doing quite well, even if he didn't have much time lately to spend with his somewhat petulant betrothed. A positively gleeful Gabi and friends made off with him to celebrate his final days as a bachelor, but I was relegated to trying on gowns and listening to endless descriptions of other peoples' weddings. The totally irrational thought of escaping to one of the plantations for a weekend haunted me. Would M. Roman mind if I suddenly showed up to just sit and unwind for a few hours on the cool verandah at Oak Alley? Of course, it wasn't going to happen, but the idea persisted.

June 30th arrived at last under clear skies. A sleepless bride greeted her wedding day with dark circles under her eyes and became the instant concern of a parade of ladies armed with assorted tricks designed to transform her into a thing of radiant beauty. Oh dear! Fortunately, breakfast was not possible because the entire family and wedding party would be receiving Holy Communion. I couldn't have eaten anyway.

The fuss continued. I was swished into every garment but the pale blue satin and seed pearl gown and made to sit still so my hair could be coiffed appropriately to accommodate the exquisite comb and Spanish lace mantilla Charles' greataunt had sent from Europe. Then came the dress. Everyone exclaimed at how gorgeous the final product was and, at last, I stood back and had a look. I must admit to having felt rather foolish at being the center of so much attention, but the image I now saw in the mirror was actually quite beautiful and a definite tribute to all the work that had gone into producing it. I did hope that Charles would be pleased and that his great adieu to the single life last evening had not been so jovially orchestrated by Gabi and friends that they would not get him to the church on time.

To say that I floated through the rest of the day as though in a dream is an understatement. Fortunately, between mention in the New Orleans Picayune and comments from family and friends, some of the details of what took place, who was there and who wore what, returned to my own foggy memory of that long awaited and swiftly spent day in June.

Courtesy of the Historic New Orleans Collection, Detail, Acc. No. 1951.72

Wedding Festivities

Courtesy of the Historic New Orleans Collection, Detail, Acc. No. 1974.25.30.728

The Final Journey

CHAPTER VII

*T*he rest of the summer proved to be rather uneventful and was spent settling into our new home, receiving daily visits from old friends and well-wishers, and relaxing on an occasional riverboat trip to St. James Parish for a welcome break from the characteristic mugginess of the city. While there, we called on the Romans and were brought up to date on what had been going on in their lives. M. Roman was in the midst of a new treatment recommended to him by Dr. Edouard Fortier. Whatever could encourage more oxygen to the lungs was considered beneficial, at least temporarily, and we commented to each other about M. Telesphore's ruddy cheeks. Was this a good sign, or a mark of the relentless fever which lately had become his constant companion? Whatever the cause, it was unnatural because not only had he hemorrhaged on several occasions, but also the poor man had been leeched in a last resort return to old remedies, thereby depleting him of what little blood he had left. How could his frail body be expected to rebuild a healthy supply? It seemed so pointless. We promised him special prayers and a Mass to be said for his intentions.

Louise told us of his often mentioned request that, when he was gone, his family not indulge themselves in deep mourning and other 'foolish customs', as he put it, which were more for show than a sign of true sorrow. It was obvious that J. T. Roman was a man of deep faith. His long illness had prepared him to endure with a sense of acceptance and peace. Louise, in particular, was deeply touched by her father's gentleness and tranquility as the days of his life dwindled away. It seemed as though there was an actual correlation between his spirit's gathering strength and the weakening of his body.

That was the last time we saw M. Roman alive. Shortly after winter turned to spring in 1848, he took his last breath. He died at his beloved Oak Alley home of only nine years with his family at his side. Though he had scoffed at the idea of traditional mourning rituals at a loved one's passing, it was impossible not to display emotion at the loss of this kind and courageous man.

Celina seemed completely shocked and in denial for weeks. She would constantly refer to Telesphore as though he were just in the other room. These moments would be followed by hours of uncontrolled sobbing and moaning. The poor lady was beside herself and none of us could help her. Gabi was deeply affected by the death of his beloved uncle. He and Valcour were constantly on hand to comfort the family and to take over business matters and funeral arrangements. Tony's letters to Gabi were shared with all and we commented on how beautifully he expressed the thoughts and words of wisdom he knew would comfort his friend.

Celina, between bouts of anguish, insisted on the most expensive and ornate materials for her husband's tomb and would listen to no one about practical matters. M. Roman's remains were placed temporarily in a tomb in New Orleans near the bodies of George and Albert, two little sons who had died in infancy some years ago, to await completion of the marble mausoleum being erected in the St. James Parish churchyard cemetery. It wasn't until January of 1849 that the *Gabriel Aime,* her port and starboard sides bearing single black wreaths, carried the remains of the three Romans, father and two sons, on a solemn journey up river to their lavishly designed final resting place. Friends and family were waiting to receive them and gathered closely around the mausoleum while the coffins were transferred from the boat.

As we waited for the entourage, Charles and I visited one or two other tombs bearing names we knew, and we stopped to say a prayer by the gated section of the cemetery where plantation slaves were buried. Near the gate we saw the newly erected, small wooden cross with the name of Celestine on it, and I remembered well what a bright and willing child she had been. In my mind's eye, I could still see her with the little vase of fresh roses she always placed near M. Roman to, as she explained, "make him happy". A victim of diphtheria, she was only 12 years old when she died, just a few weeks before her master found peace at last. She, too, rested in consecrated ground, not far from him.

Such a fragile thing life is. Master or slave, young or old, how quickly it is spent! Standing in the cemetery that day, I felt the bond between time and eternity, and was surprised to find that deep sorrow had been replaced with a sense of peace and reassurance. In a flash, it became clear to me that it was this certainty that M. Telesphore had known all along, and that the day would surely come when I, too, would need it to draw strength from.

As the iron gates closed heavily on the tomb, we each whispered one last adieu to a good friend, and drifted quietly back toward the road and waiting carriages.

TO THE
MEMORY OF
Minerva P. Turner
Who died,
Oct. 25.th 1845.
Aged 34 yr.s.
7 months, & 6 days.

Courtesy of the Historic New Orleans Collection, Detail, Acc. No. 1957.124.33

Rest in Peace

Daughters Are Presented to Society

Courtesy of the Historic New Orleans Collection, Detail, Acc. No. 1951.74

CHAPTER VIII

*W*hen Celina had quite exhausted herself with the long list of mourning rituals and constant stream of visitors determined to 'console' her with lurid tales of the woes of widowhood, she withdrew to the room at the head of the stairs where her husband had been cared for during his last days. She refused to get out of bed and insisted that the children stay with her for hours at a time to share her grief. Tante Jo spoke to her about this and reminded her of Telesphore's almost passionate demands that his family, especially the children, not be submitted to the excesses of traditional mourning customs; that true feeling is in the heart, not on the back. Indeed, he had ordered that these very words be recorded in his will. Celina, of course, would have none of it and screeched through another barrage of tears and wailing that Tante Jo was heartless and incapable of understanding her grief.

It seemed to completely elude the almost deranged widow that Tante Jo had lost her beloved baby brother and was deeply grieved as well. Mother and I shared the thought that Tante Jo must have felt resentment for the way Celina had acted during Telesphore's illness and agonizing last days, but she shouldered her own sadness in silence and revealed nothing beyond her determined efforts to console Celina and the now fatherless children.

Valcour and his brother-in-law, André, assumed the immediate affairs of the estate, later delegating the firm of Roman and Kernion to supervise matters until the succession should become completely solvent and easily manageable. This awesome group of businessmen and financial wizards did all they could to prepare for the day when Celina would, as she insisted, finally be permitted to take over as sole executrix and would no longer have to render accounts to anyone. The idea of such a scenario was most unsettling to all members of the family. Celina had no concept of how to handle expenses, nor did she understand that the plantation crops would only continue to provide her with income as long as care was taken to re-invest in the upkeep, and in continual development of innovative and efficient techniques for optimum production. Her husband's last will and testament made it clear that he did not feel Celina was at all prepared to assume charge of any phase of the business. He expected an appropriate person, his brother, André, for one, to be at the helm until such time that his son or future sons-in-law might be of an age and understanding to assume responsibility of family affaires. Time alone would tell, but for the next few years it remained for the brothers Roman and Valcour Aime to keep a vigilant eye on Oak Alley matters and on Celina's expenditures.

During the years between 1849 and 1855, the succession of J. T. Roman was rendered completely solvent, thanks to the careful management of those in charge, but Celina lived for the time when she would be free at last to spend lavishly on anything she wanted. She felt the need to indulge in all manner of extravagances, both in town and at the plantation. She already kept numerous carriages and fine horses so that she could ride up and down River Road visiting friends and relatives during her summers at Oak Alley, and immersed herself in the pursuit of an extraordinarily active city social life as well. She was tireless in her efforts to see that her daughters were received in all the best circles. Suitable husbands would eventually be found for all three, and the completion of Henri's education, both here and abroad had to be assured. There was much to do, and Celina did not intend to let grass grow beneath *her* feet. As always, easy credit prevailed in a thriving economy. A family name associated with wealth was all that was needed to qualify for almost unlimited funds, and Celina was quick to acquaint herself with eager money lenders who would be satisfied with her signature alone. Her brother-in-law, André, was continually frustrated by her complete disregard of attempted guidance and arguments for the prudence of curtailing her incessant spending. Finally, he could take no more. By January of 1855, he was to sideline his serious misgivings and relinquish the reins to a possessive 39 year old Celina.

Everyone marked Celina's concern that Louise, the eldest, had not yet become a bride, nor did she seem anxious to show any preference for the young men in her social circles. Louise was noted for her beauty and intelligence and more than one suitor was observed calling on her during the family's prolonged stays in the city, but she encouraged no one in particular. There was time, she would tell her mother, and she felt she could do more to help at home for the moment. The truth was that, although her defense of her mother remained firm, she was inwardly disturbed by Celina's penchant for extravagance. Admittedly, it wasn't easy to stay ahead of Celina when she was determined to do one thing or another, but it could be worse if she were left on her own with no supervision at all.

That Louise's sister, Octavie, met Philip "Buck" Buchanan, an American, and had fallen in love was not quite what Celina had in mind for her either. It bothered her that Philip was not a Creole, but at least his father was Judge Alexandre Buchanan and his family a distinguished one, albeit from the other side of Canal Street. Octavie would look at no others anyway, so the marriage of the two young people was accepted as inevitable and a date was set for the wedding to take place a year later. However, destiny would have it otherwise, for a series of tragic events were about to take place which would call for the indefinite postponement of Octavie and Buck's nuptials. In fact, it wouldn't be until December of 1858 that the two finally exchanged vows at St. Louis Cathedral, amid much elegance.

Courtesy of the Historic New Orleans Collection, Detail, Acc. No. 1955.45

In the Vieux Carre

CHAPTER IX

*M*eanwhile, things at our Rue Iberville address buzzed with activity. In May of 1850 Charles and I had welcomed our first child, a daughter whom we named Marie Josephine. By September of the following year there was a son, René, and signs of yet another pregnancy had become manifest not too long after. Babies, nannies and getting through the ever changing obstacle course of childcare took top priority in our lives. To say we had little time to visit friends and family in the River Parishes during this almost continual yearly expansion of our family is an understatement. We longed for a time when we could pack up the whole household and move upriver for an entire summer away from those inevitable sticky days and nights in the city.

By late March of 1854 the unusually long list of names in the newspaper's death notices had become the main topic of conversation. People were becoming uneasy. It was noised about that even Dufilho Pharmacy on Rue Chartres was hard pressed to keep its ample shelves stocked with medical supplies, so great was the demand. Some optimistically observed that the winter, though it had been a strangely mild one, was still evident. It wasn't the time of year when one might tend to relate an increase in deaths among residents of the more elite neighborhoods with recent gossip about a "bad fever sickness" stalking the dilapidated outskirts of the city. Or was it? New Orleanians were certainly no strangers to the horror of unpredictable killer diseases such as yellow fever and malaria. Few families could say they had not lost at least one loved one to this frightening summer time curse. Continued daily reports of deaths kept people close to their homes while the topic of conversation turned more and more to what remedies were best indicated for prevention and/or cure of all manner of possible ills, both real and imagined. Finally, as paranoia increased throughout the city, many people felt driven to seek refuge in the country.

By April, the heat had already begun to build and it was clear that we were in for an extremely unpleasant summer, with storms and rains keeping every moment humid, sweltering and mosquito filled. Added to our physical discomfort were daily reports of new cases of malaria. An increased number of deaths had now been attributed beyond any doubt to yellow fever. That being the case, Charles and I had not a moment's hesitation in accepting the Aimes' invitation to join them at the plantation until late September when some relief might be expected. Besides, we were anxious to be there to welcome Gabi when he returned from his latest trip to Europe. Seeing him again was going to be such fun and we looked forward to hearing all about his travels. Not only would we see Gabi, but our dear friend Tony was also expected to form part of the welcoming committee. Tony was now Father Antoine Josef, and we were told that he had been granted leave before departing for his first missionary assignment among the Miskito Indians on the east coast of Nicaragua.

Our boisterous group arrived at Le Petit Versailles on May 12th, just before little Marie Jo's 4th birthday. Tony wasn't expected until September, and there were no other house guests at the time, so we expanded gloriously on the shaded verandah, strolled with Edwige and Florent and their children on the levee, or just sat quietly with Tante Jo and Oncle Valcour while they filled us in on all the latest family news.

Celina and the children had been at Oak Alley since late April. We visited them several times and found them in good health and enjoying the fresh air of the country. It was so much more peaceful than it had been during the last month or so in town, and we rested contentedly as the lazy days drifted by. Marie Jo's birthday was celebrated under the trees. Besides the Fortier children, Tante Jo had invited some of the grandchildren of about the same age, and the day was so exciting that we had trouble getting the birthday child to settle down at bedtime. She kept bouncing out of bed as she remembered this moment or that and ran her nanny quite ragged chasing after her. Well, even the adults had enjoyed the day, and we knew Marie Jo would remember it always.

Excitement always followed Gabi's latest letters from Europe. His vivid accounts of visits to famous sites, and his new experiences abroad were shared with all at evening gatherings in the parlor. Every letter was directed to those he had been told were gathered at Le Petit Versailles, including Charles and me. He made valiant attempts to delight the ladies with brief descriptions of the latest fashion trends and hinted at some of the more interesting scandals. He said he'd been shopping and had a case full of surprises he hoped would please. He wrote he had heard from Tony and that mid September had been confirmed for his return to Louisiana.

Of course, all Gabi's sisters anxiously awaited their brother's return, but Felicie, closest to him in age, was ecstatic. Each time she and her husband, Alfred, visited her parents, she would unlock Gabi's room so she could see just exactly how he had left it the day he departed on this last trip to Europe. She said Tante Jo would let no one change a thing because she wanted Gabi to find his room as though he had never been away. I'd remind her that she'd already given us the grand tour several times, but she would laugh and eagerly pull me from this corner of the room to that, lovingly fingering a cravat clip, his comb and silver backed brush, or the elegant fencing sword with which he had earned several awards for his skills. She was proud that he kept a small lithograph of her on his desk and told me she was counting the days until he was home. Indeed, so were we all. I told Charles about the many wonderful times I'd shared with Gabi as we were growing up, and Charles contributed some rather hilarious accounts of their school days together. Was it really true that Gabi once locked the sacristan in the school church belfry and then walked nonchalantly by, greeting in friendly fashion the wildly waving victim of his prank as he peered out from his perch in the steeple? Charles assured me that not only was it so, but also that it was one of several adventures admiringly recalled by the student body.

Courtesy of the Historic New Orleans Collection, Detail, Acc. No. 1981.216.ii

Angels of Mercy

CHAPTER X

*J*uly steamed its way into a seething August. The temperature rarely dropped below 90 degrees, even at night, and reports from the city were ominous. Many more cases of yellow fever had been diagnosed, and the death rate soared with the passing of each hot, sticky day. Afternoon storms did little but stir up the humidity and voracious mosquitos, and we were so glad we could be at the plantation.

It wasn't until late afternoon on September 16th that a lone figure in full soutane appeared heading up the pathway toward the house. Charles had been seated on the porch trying to catch a breeze or two off the river, and was the first to see the visitor. It took him no more than a second to recognize Tony, and with a shout of joy, he ran out to meet his old friend. I saw them both from the window and flew down the stairs just as they came through the door.

Father Antoine Josef stood before us at last, and hugs and excited babbling immediately surrounded him.

Tante Jo heard the commotion and came out to greet him, followed by Valcour, vigorously swatting with his riding crop the dust accumulated on his boots from his after tea gallop over the grounds. What a joyous reunion! We proudly presented the children to Father Tony. They were so instantly captivated by him that a squabble erupted about who was to be allowed to sit on his lap as he brought us up to date on all that had been going on in his life. He had been ordained last July and, as we knew, had received his first missionary assignment. The entire household gathered in the parlor before dinner for a special Rosary of thanksgiving for the safe return of Tony and for Gabi's arrival tomorrow.

I got the children to bed and then went to the porch where the others were sipping iced drinks and fanning themselves as they absorbed all the news Tony had gleaned from his companions on the boat ride from St. Louis, as well as reports from brother priests serving in the most seriously affected areas of New Orleans. He told us the situation was very bad indeed, and that the fever had reached epidemic proportions.

Tony promised that he would wait over until Gabi's arrival, then would go on to see his family in Donaldsonville. His parents and four brothers had already visited him in St. Louis, and were there for his ordination and celebration of his first Holy Mass, but it had been a long time and he knew they would be anxious to see him.

We talked almost to midnight before turning in. Tony was to be lodged in the garçonniere on the side of the house nearest Gabi's room, and there were other guests expected for the welcoming who would soon fill the other side. In addition to the large suite occupied by Oncle Valcour and Tante Jo, and the ample living quarters for Edwige and Florent Fortier and their children, the house had a great number of smaller bedrooms, and those, plus the garçonnieres, would be packed by well-wishers.

The *Gabriel Aime* had already been dispatched to New Orleans where Gabi, who had been there since the 14th, would board her for his final lap home. Valcour had word that she was due to round the bend in the river no later than mid-afternoon of the 17th. There was no doubt that by tomorrow at daybreak, the household would be in an uproar of joyful preparations; children running hither and yon, panting nannies chasing them in frustration, vases of flowers on every table, and sounds and aromas from the kitchen indicating the high level of the feast being created under André's supervision. All was designed to gladden the heart of the returning voyager.

The sun had barely cleared the tree tops when the entire plantation grounds, as well as the length and breadth of the levee before it, were festooned, adorned, and arranged to accommodate the groups of welcomers. House guests and callers from nearby plantations began gathering just before noon, and refreshments were continually provided throughout the ensuing vigil. Valcour had dispatched sentinels on horseback to the downriver curve of the levee so they could sound the alarm as soon as the *Gabriel Aime* was sighted.

It surely was hot! But a breeze would puff up now and then to cool us off, and we had all dressed in light cotton wherever possible. No frock coats for the gentlemen today! White shirts and rolled up sleeves were in order, and the tables set up with iced drinks and delicate snacks helped to refresh the gathering until Gabi arrived or the sun began to set, whichever came first.

At last we heard the signal. She was coming around the bend. We all ran to the crest of the levee to wait for her. Little Marie Jo saw her first, and squealed with delight as she skipped about while pointing downstream at the tall stack and gleaming bow of the *Gabriel Aime*. From the calliope could be faintly heard one of Stephen Foster's latest tunes, and the gathering buzzed in happy anticipation, each one wishing to be the first to see Gabi waving from the deck as he drew nearer and nearer.

He didn't seem to be there, though. In fact, it wasn't until the boat had docked that we saw him step out of the salon and move toward the gangplank. What was wrong? This wasn't like Gabi. He should have been returning our waves and shouts, and dancing to the music like a delighted child. Those of us nearest the dock saw Valcour embrace him, then hold him back at arms' length to get a better look.

It was clear to us that he didn't like what he saw. Tante Jo hugged him tightly and was so happy she noticed little else but that her boy was home. He smiled at everyone and started slowly down the gangplank. Now we were really concerned. Gabi looked so haggard and disheveled. He hadn't even bothered to shave, and it looked almost like he staggered at one point as he stepped off onto the levee. He couldn't be drunk! He was always a most meticulous person in his habits and his dress. He did his best to greet the welcoming crowd and then turned to hug Tony with an almost frightening display of emotion. Well, he was just tired, he said, and would be fine as soon as he had a chance to relax a bit and cool off. The city had been merciless with heat, he told us, and it took a great deal out of one. We accepted this explanation, but I saw Tony and Charles exchange glances and wondered what they wanted to say to each other.

The crowd accompanied Gabi to the front porch of the house where Marc was waiting for him with a cool drink. Marc asked if he would like to have a change of clothes laid out that would be more comfortable, but Gabi said he'd just sit there for awhile. Shortly after, I noticed Matthew, charged with seeing to Tony's needs, exchanging some sort of guarded conversation with Marc. I'd heard earlier that they had fussed at each other over who was to be valet to Gabi. Simon made them draw straws and Marc won, but Matt was more than tickled to learn that it was he who would be assigned to the needs of none other than

Father Antoine Josef. In any case, I knew both of them far too well to doubt their ability to uncover whatever mystery had disembarked with Gabi, and made a mental note to interrogate one of them at the first opportunity.

At dinner time, I still had not been able to corner either Matt or Marc. By now, Gabi was visibly exhausted, and even though the table was laden with his favorite foods, he begged to be excused so that he could go to bed and get some rest. Tomorrow was another day, he said, and there would be plenty of time to visit. I felt a lump in my throat as I watched Gabi, with Marc in attendance, drag himself up the stairs to his room. Perhaps he was right. Maybe all he needed was a good night's sleep in his own bed. It had certainly been a long day for him.

Tante Jo and Oncle Valcour went about the business of presiding over the sumptuous dinner and the musical entertainment which followed. Emma had prepared an aria which she had heard Jenny Lind sing in New Orleans during her celebrated visit three years before. What a beautiful performance it was! We hoped his sister's lovely voice would penetrate Gabi's dreams just a little, since it was all for him. We made Emma promise to repeat the aria tomorrow, after Gabi was rested and feeling more like himself. Tante Jo ran upstairs once to check in on him, reported him sound asleep, and continued with her duties as gracious hostess.

It was close to midnight when the last carriage disappeared down the road. The house guests had all retired, and Charles and I went up stairs to our room at the left of the landing. Everything seemed quiet, the children were asleep and their nannies taking turns as vigils. It had been exciting and wonderful to see Gabi, but strange. Well, we would be together tomorrow at breakfast and would find out what was going on. We turned out the lamp and drifted off to sleep.

Yellow Fever Victim

Courtesy of the Historic New Orleans Collection, Detail, Acc. No. 1981.216.ii

CHAPTER XI

*W*e were awakened in the morning by the most heart-rending cry that I had ever heard. Charles sprang from bed and ran into the hall with me in close pursuit. There was such commotion that it was hard to take everything in, but I could see that Gabi's door was ajar. Tony was already running up the stairs and I followed him and Charles down the hall to where the entire household seemed to be gathering. There was an upturned tray on the floor by the bed, a red rose still in the broken vase beside it. Valcour was lying face down over Gabi's still body, and Tante Jo was hugging him and sobbing. Not one thing made any sense to me, least of all that Marc had his arms around his brother and was moaning over and over, "c'est mort ... he's dead!" Charles grabbed them both and demanded to know what was going on. Marc had enormous trouble composing himself, but finally could relate that Simon, himself, had taken Gabi's breakfast tray into the room and was about to place it on the bed while he, Marc, was busy preparing his bath and wardrobe for the day. As Simon leaned forward to put the tray down, he said "bon jour" softly, but Gabi didn't move. Touching his shoulder, Simon turned him slightly and it was then that he cried out, dropped the tray, and ran to call his master.

There was nothing more to tell. Yellow fever had claimed another victim, our Gabi. He was no more. It seemed that time stood still and, were it not for the heart broken sobbing and lamenting, I would have sworn it was all a ghastly nightmare.

Tony had sent Matthew for his case and was preparing to anoint Gabi's still warm body. He prayed fervently that his dear friend was already at peace. Valcour was of more immediate concern. Tante Jo was being tended by Edwige and a large retinue of ladies, but Valcour remained almost catatonic. He would respond to no one, and knelt staring at Gabi while Tony sadly ministered to his dear friend. No weeping, no noise, just the silence of a heart shattered beyond repair.

At last Gabi, now dressed and laid out for the wake, was ready to receive the final farewells from a long, long line of mourners. Valcour would not move from his son's side. At one point he asked Simon to bring him his diary. On the page marked September 18, 1854, Valcour penned his last entry: "Let him who wishes continue. My time is done - he died on September 18. I kissed him at five o'clock, also on the following day ..." He sealed this entry with wax. His will to live had vanished, never to return.

At twenty-eight years of age, Gabi was gone. The tall, handsome, wonderful friend of my youth had exchanged time for eternity. We who were left were stunned. None of us would ever be the same - Valcour, least of all.

Tony was to celebrate a Requiem Mass early the next morning and the funeral procession would then proceed the seven and a half miles up River Road to the cemetery where Gabi would rest beside the others. Later, as we stood once again among the marble tombs, Charles and I shared the sad thought that we were beginning to count more of our loved ones in this spot than in life.

We could not get Valcour's tragic face out of our minds. His only son and heir, gone. There would be no more direct descendants bearing the Aime name. No son of Gabi would play in the beautiful gardens or wage battles from the fort, with stockpiles of oranges in lieu of canon balls. There would be no bright eyed boy to spin wild tales about Old 'Roo and his trip from New South Wales, no pirates or knights in armor, or the excitement of an attack from poltergeists at midnight. Just memories remained. I made a vow then and there to somehow keep them all fresh, and to share them with those who might also remember, and would smile.

Courtesy of the Historic New Orleans Collection, Detail, Acc. No. 1974.25.30.722

Farewell

CHAPTER XII

*T*ony stayed by Valcour's side as long as he could. They would sit facing each other, heads bowed close together as they shared heavy thoughts, and drew deeply upon their rich faith that promised them that their Gabi was never more alive than now, and that he had just gone on ahead. They prayed together, and as a family. Shortly before Tony's departure, we gathered to open the case of promised gifts Gabi had spoken of in his letters. With tears streaming down our cheeks we passed from hand to hand the carefully selected souvenirs of his last European journey, savoring the significance of each before sharing it with another. Some of the more whimsical of his purchases even brought smiles through the tears, but, one and all, they reflected the bright spirit of him whom we so sorely missed.

We looked up as Marc entered the room with a large rectangular package wrapped in brown paper and tied with string. He laid it in Valcour's lap and said he'd found it propped in a corner near Gabi's bed. It had been with the rest of the luggage which had been taken to the room shortly following Gabi's arrival, but had been forgotten in all that had transpired. Valcour lovingly stroked the package, meditating on what this additional gift might be that Gabi reckoned would please his loved ones. Slowly, he untied the string and tore the paper off. A harsh sob escaped from his throat as he looked down on a portrait of Gabi in a carved wooden frame ... a portrait he sat for during the days spent in New Orleans before boarding the *Gabriel Aime* for the river trip home. We were transfixed, unable to say or do anything, as the stricken faces of Valcour and Tante Jo gazing at the portrait of their dead son, were etched in our memories forever. Unbidden, an ironic thought crossed my mind. Had Gabi not lingered in town to sit for the portrait, he might have escaped the illness that claimed his life.

That night, as I struggled with so many unanswered questions to the events of the past few days, the memory of my mother's words about the inevitability of joys and sorrows going hand in hand through our lives brought back bedtime stories she shared with me many years ago, and I bowed once again to her wisdom.

It worried Charles and me to think of what Tante Jo, Valcour and the girls would do once Tony had to leave. We had promised our parents that we would remain with the

Aimes as long as they might need our support, but it could never be the same without Tony.

The moment came at last for us to say goodbye to him, and there was nothing we could do about it. Tony gave us all his blessing, promised to let us know about his trip to Nicaragua, and assured us that we would all be in his Holy Masses every single day. We would see each other again, he said. Time would go fast. We would see that it was so.

Oh, dear Tony, how we wanted you to stay and give us strength!

Courtesy of the Historic New Orleans Collection, Detail, Acc. No. 1955.45

Return to the City

CHAPTER XIII

*A*t last it was time for us to return to the city. The worst was now over and no new cases of fever had been reported. The weather had cooled to frosty mornings, and we had much to catch up on at home. Fortunately, our families had survived in good health, and we spent many hours with them reliving the sadness of the Aimes family tragedy. As soon as it was clear that they were not carriers of the dread disease, Mother and Father went to be with their old friends. There they stayed through the bitter-sweetness of the Christmas Season, and into the new year. Upon their return, they described the situation at Le Petit Versailles. How sorely grieved we were to learn of the relentless unwinding of the golden thread of life of that once joyous family! We prayed that time, the legendary healer of pain, would do its job before it was too late to matter.

It seemed, though, that Valcour was determined to

disappear within himself. He went from agonized grief to numbness, and then to what almost seemed indifference to anything or anyone around him. Even his beloved Jo became little more than a shadow at his side. She tried to interest him in things that once intrigued him, but he would only pat her arm gently, call her "petite Josephine", and forget she was there. Did he not see that she, too, was devastated with grief? The girls tried to comfort their parents, but could do little to keep them from slipping further and further away from reality.

Florent's role shifted from son-in-law/assistant to that of chief administrator of the entire business operation. Fortunately, an excellent working plan had long been in effect, due entirely to Valcour's farsightedness and keen business sense, so the only real burden facing the family was that of Valcour's struggle within himself as he edged dangerously close to the deadly quicksand of despair.

The saddest part was that he had so isolated himself that his loved ones were unable to know his deepest thoughts. Two years later, when he had finally come to terms with Gabi's death, it was too late. In February of 1857, poor, sweet Tante Jo died of a broken heart. Her death was followed shortly by the loss of little Felicie. In the end, of the charming, vivacious, and immediate family circle, only Valcour and his three eldest daughters remained. Valcour's answer was to retire to the seclusion of an old ice house near by. He took with him some candles, his Rosary beads, a prayer book, and the portrait of Gabi.

He told the girls that he would not be far and asked that they not concern themselves. He assured them he would be fine. He just needed solitude and a spiritual retreat. We know he cherished the memory of each word of comfort Tony had shared with him, and though they were few and far between, his letters from Nicaragua brought much solace to the tormented man.

Then, suddenly, on a grey March morning of that same year, just weeks before her 17th birthday, the household was thrust once again into deep mourning when Marie Roman died at the Roman home in New Orleans after a brief illness. Celina's shock and disbelief echoed her intense suffering following her husband's demise only a few years before and once more we gathered around to offer our support and whatever assistance she would accept. Yet again, close friends and family boarded the *Gabriel Aime* to accompany Marie's black-shrouded coffin back to St. James, where she would join her father and little brothers. A completely disconsolate Celina decided that she and the children would stay nearby at Oak Alley throughout the summer months, while both plantations remained shrouded in mourning.

Courtesy of the Historic New Orleans Collection, Detail, Acc. No. 1953.29

Slave labor

CHAPTER XIV

*L*ater that year we learned that Tony's mission in Nicaragua had been interrupted. He was to come back to New Orleans and, at Charles' request, was granted permission to stay with us so he would be near medical assistance and could fully recover from his many hardships and near fatal bout with cholera. While we anxiously awaited more news, Charles answered some of my questions about the circumstances leading to Tony's return. He explained to me that Nicaragua was a country whose importance to the United States had become critical, due to its potential for a coast to coast canal through the Rio San Juan. It was a large country, stretching from coast to coast, and contained vast and often unchartered jungle areas where every man had to fend for himself. From what Charles had been told, Tony, cut off from his mission headquarters in Greytown by ever increasing outbreaks of guerilla warfare, had worked endless hours assisting the wounded and dying among the forces of that famous filibuster and soldier of fortune from Tennessee, William Walker. Walker's once powerful army of volunteers sent to back up a local revolution, had been decimated by disease and constant attacks from the opposition in the struggle between liberal nationalists and conservative advocates of a plan to turn Nicaragua into a slave state.

Inevitably, Tony, himself, fell victim to the terribly debilitating cholera, and had he not found shelter with a Miskito family skilled in the art of herbal remedies, he would have died.

Following Walker's recent agreement to the terms of President Buchanan's truce, a United States warship was sent to transport him and his staff back to New Orleans. Charles learned that, at Walker's personal request, a bedraggled Tony was to be included on board.

The day the ship put in to port, Walker was received as a hero with much pomp and glowing speeches. Amid the fanfare, few even noticed the presence of a frail and haggard priest as he was assisted by Charles down the gangplank and to our home where he could rest and garner much needed strength before joining his brother priests and, no doubt, receiving a new assignment.

During the time spent recuperating with us, Tony shared some of his experiences. Many an evening after dinner I would join the men in the drawing room where, my needlework lying untouched in my lap, I would listen as

Tony described the confusion and chaos resulting from the see-sawing of political interests between liberals and conservatives, proponents of slavery and those in total opposition, large investments by those in the United States anxious to get in on the ground floor of the location of a coast to coast canal, and the Nicaraguan resistence to foreign interference in an on going struggle for autonomy. He spoke of Vanderbilt's successes in opening up stage coach travel through the country and the dissension between him and Walker, of the church's efforts in support of the conservatives, of Walker's amazing ability to rally forces behind him, and even his brief tenure as president of Nicaragua. Tony said he doubted very much, given the extraordinary intellect of the man, that the world had seen the last of William Walker. He certainly was greatly admired by slave owners throughout the south, who evidently chose to forget that he had once declared himself against the concept of human bondage. Also, it was a well known fact that Central American countries had renounced slavery the moment they won independence from Spain, but where there is a demand for something there will be a supply one way or another, and slaves, as well as other commodities, formed part of a busy world market. Very volatile times, indeed!

Missionary work was as demanding as it was rewarding, and Tony knew there was much for him to do as soon as he could get back on his feet. There was no doubt that his life had been hard. He was only 33 and his hair was almost completely white.

Tony did not fully recuperate until the early part of 1858. He stayed with us for many months, and then returned to St. Louis to complete the mending of his battered body. As always, we missed him and wished he could have been part of the family longer, but duty called, and he had to leave.

CHAPTER XV

*D*uring the summer of 1859, another disaster struck the heart of the Roman/Aime families, this time at Oak Alley. Celina and Louise had retreated to the country as usual, and were relaxing after the social rush surrounding Octavie and Buck's wedding. Louise, much to her mother's delight, had been receiving rather frequent visits from a suitor whose family members numbered among the better known River Region plantation owners and who were reputed to be quite distinguished, if somewhat given to overindulgence in rich foods and fine wines.

One afternoon, shortly before tea time, the gentleman appeared at the door and asked for Mademoiselle Louise. He was expected, he said, and would wait in the hall. Louise descended the staircase with her usual poise and went to welcome her visitor. As he bowed and approached her, it became all too clear that he was most definitely 'in his cups'. In fact, he nearly tripped over a chair. Louise was furious. She spun about, snapped her fan open, and started back up the stairs. Half way up the first flight she slipped. Her fall broke one of the bone stays of her hoop skirt and the jagged edge pierced her leg, seriously wounding her. So determined was she to escape her visitor that she vehemently refused any assistance, and dragged herself up to her room and locked the door. She would speak to no one, not even her mother, and it was impossible to know how badly she was hurt. By the time her condition had reached the point where she could no longer manage the pain, gangrene had set in. Louise faced a life or death situation. The family returned to New Orleans where Dr. Alfred Mercier, a well known surgeon, examined Louise and announced that it was too late to save her leg. Amputation was the only way to save 24 year old Louise's life, and it had to be performed immediately at the Circus Street Hospital.

Poor Louise! In an instant her whole future did an about face. Had it not been for her deep faith and strength of character, she would have turned from life itself. As it was, she forced herself to become as independent as possible and, ultimately, became the sole companion of Celina's waning years. Her amputated limb was buried in a tomb already prepared for the day when its owner would join it to await Final Judgement and resurrection of the dead.

CHAPTER XVI

*M*eanwhile, ominous rumblings of secession were becoming louder as the South's grip on slavery tightened in fear. How could the huge plantations continue without slave labor? Once again, Valcour's history of astuteness became apparent when his books revealed the amazing fact that, not only was Le Petit Versailles set up to function with or without slavery, but also that it had been in the process of converting to a non-slave arrangement for the harvesting and processing of the Aime's huge sugar crop and diverse agricultural commodities. Although Valcour, himself, was still in deep mourning and remained mostly on the periphery of general activities, his plantation was already primed to withstand the most trying of times that were yet to befall the southland, in general, and the River Region, in particular.

Patient as ever with my unending questions about what was going on and how it might affect us or our friends, Charles explained to me that local planters had originally opposed secession from the Union, and that André Roman had been one of the seventeen delegates to vote against the ordinance of secession on January 26, 1861. Nevertheless, once Louisiana's secession could no longer be avoided, the Aime and Roman families stood in loyal support, both financially and with soldiers and statesmen, for her and for the Confederacy. Governor Roman was one of three Confederate commissioners sent in early spring to Washington to negotiate a peaceable division of the country. However, President Lincoln refused recognition to them on April 8, 1861, and on April 12th, Gen. P.G.T. Beauregard of New Orleans, opened fire on Ft. Sumter. War was no longer a threat. It was reality.

The onset of Civil War seemed to spike Valcour out of seclusion and into a degree of action. After the fall of New Orleans in April of 1862, Federal troops added insult to injury by bombarding and sacking plantations. Though some fared worse than others during these hideous raids, none were spared completely. Even folks at Oak Alley reported an occasional frightening rain of shells which, fortunately, fell short of the house and the farthest fields, where people were huddled in terror. At Le Petit Versailles, Florent and Edwige's son also described later how he and the family hid in the shelter of the levee as shells flew over their heads and landed all over the plantation grounds. The house was not hit, but terror reigned throughout the once peaceful countryside. War touched everyone in the land one way or another. Blue or Gray, it didn't really matter what color uniform young men wore. They left their homes and loved ones with the same heavy hearts, all too many of them never to return.

Charles, despite my wild protestations and reminders that he was a family man with responsibilities right here, was one of the first to go. He served his beloved Confederacy under none other than General P. G. T. Beauregard. Of the full time of his service, he returned but once on a short leave, and then could only offer weak attempts at hope for the future. He was gone as quickly as he had appeared, handsome and brave, but no longer optimistic.

Time, as we have seen, goes by. One day followed another into history, and then news began to spread throughout the city that the end was near. It is sad to recall that my prayers were no longer for the glory of the Confederacy, but just that the whole horrible thing be over. So we lost the war! All that mattered was that Charles would soon be home again.

It was not to be. The double-edged sword of life drove steel into my heart when, on what I will forever recall as the darkest day in the year 1864, a soldier clad in a tattered gray uniform knocked on our door, bowed and presented me with a sealed document. I remember backing away from him in horror, and the awareness that I already knew what the document would reveal. It seemed to my non-functioning brain that if I didn't look at it, it wouldn't be so. The poor young man before me was almost beside himself with embarrassment and I realized that I had to gather my wits, thank him, and let him go. Trembling, I sat in a chair near the window and slowly read the words I'd hoped and prayed would never be addressed to me: Charles, my dearest friend and gentle, loving husband, had been killed in action near Petersburg, Virginia. The battle had been fierce, and he had died a hero (had not they all?). He had been buried where he fell, there being no other possible option. He was decorated posthumously by Gen. Beauregard, himself, who personally presented me with Charles' sabre and with his medals.

And so, not a year before General Lee's surrender, I found myself left with the memory of 17 happy years of marriage, our children, and a measure of comfort to be found in sharing it all with a few dear old friends who had managed to survive the unspeakable horrors of civil war.

I wrote Tony, of course, and was consoled by his assurance that he would come to be with us shortly. He reminded me that Charles is, after all, only a heart beat away. Tony, himself, had never been able to completely regain his strength, and was not only allowed extended leave, but also was told he would not be returning to missionary duties. He was disappointed, but we were not! As always, the children and I savored each moment with him, and would find courage in his presence and in his solid trust in God. We knew he would help heal the open wounds, but there were to be vivid scars left behind that could never fade.

Why does mankind inflict this sort of misery on himself? What, in the end, has been gained? What progress made? The abolishment of slavery? Granted, this was an evil that had to be eliminated, but I looked about in wonder at what began to take its place. It was called "sharecropping", and seemed to me to be little improvement over the other. Even as bondsmen, their masters had at least assumed the responsibility of seeing to their needs and well being. Now, bewildered and lost, they faced a land laid waste by war, and a once thriving community so devastated that it had absolutely nothing to fill an out-stretched hand or an empty stomach. These former slaves were now forced to provide for themselves and for their families on their own, and although they were considered free men, too many of them found themselves still hopelessly enslaved, this time by poverty.

Well, we were all poor now. Small pleasures which so many of us had taken for granted were no longer available. Once thriving city shops, if they were to fill empty shelves at all, offered scanty goods priced, for the most part, beyond our means. Our gentle life had been sharply redefined in most basic terms, none of them easy, but endurance demanded that we adjust one day at a time.

Fortunately for us, 1866 fashion trends from Europe seemed to favor a more stringent use of the yards of material once lavished upon huge hoop skirts and petticoats. A thing called a bustle was considered fashionable. It was supposed to enhance the popular tiny waist and ample bosom stressed in Europe's haute courture's latest creations. A goodly amount of material was still needed, but hoops were gone in favor of one version or another of this hump-like thing at the rear over which were draped ruffles. The ladies eagerly welcomed any change of dress other than the worn and re-worn outfits they had made do with for so long. Bonnets were, as always, quite fetching affairs, and, of course, the parasol added brightness to otherwise drab surroundings.

It was time to move on. Even the old city sighed in resignation, gathered the shards of broken dreams about her and once again faced an uncertain future. She had already survived hundreds of years of fortune's vagaries. She would still be there when we were all gone. Fine old lady! She had heart and deep roots. Not even war would get her down for long. The children and I were content to experience the recovery along with her, where we and others like us had always been at home.

CHAPTER XVII

*L*ouise Roman had made it known the year before that her intentions were to enter a discalced Carmelite order located in St. Louis. Much concern was stirred amongst the family regarding this announcement, partly because of Celina's failing health and need of Louise's presence, and partly because headstrong Louise just didn't seem the right material for a disciplined religious life. In any case, Louise remained firm in her decision, but agreed to stay with her mother and help her as long as was needed. This was really not the best time for changes. Then, too, her brother, Henri, had suffered financially and the plantation was only a step away from the auction block. Oncle André had died suddenly while strolling along a New Orleans street, and his estate inventory revealed that he, like so many others, carried a sizeable debt. Celina recalled the many times her brother-in-law had admonished her for reckless spending;

his endless lectures on the imprudence of living beyond one's means, and made no secret of her satisfaction upon learning of his misfortune. That his debts were incurred not through self-indulgence, but rather by frantic efforts to survive the war and reconstruction, did not occur to her. To the end, her resentment of André's efforts to carry out his brother's wishes was an obsession that drove her further and further away from those who might dare to challenge her aspirations.

Henri tried valiantly to hold on to the plantation, but it was just a matter of time before he would be forced to yield to his creditors. Finally, unable to make payment on the most basic notes, he relinquished his dream of perpetuating Roman ownership, and in March of 1866, signed the property over to his creditors, amongst whom were his uncle, Valcour, as well as his sisters and dying mother. These were diminished by one when, two days later, Celina joined the family's long list of deceased members. It was no surprise to anyone that her entire legacy consisted of a serious and diverse number of debts.

There was nothing left to do. I read the announcement of the public auction of Oak Alley in the Daily Picayune, and was deeply saddened. At least, Octavie and Buck were to stay on with their children for awhile, since it appeared that the new owner was not particularly interested in the property as a residence, and was probably relieved to have Buck manage things, at least temporarily. That being the case, I hoped to have another opportunity to visit them and recapture some sweet memories of better times under the beautiful oaks.

But not even that was to be. Octavie died suddenly not long after, leaving Buck with their four motherless children to carry on however they could. Now, only Henri was left in this world, for Louise had already withdrawn to the cloister. She was to return later to New Orleans as Mother Superior of a convent which soon was thriving with over two hundred sisters within its walls, but it was nevertheless a fact that the hopes and dreams of Jacques Telesphore and Celina Roman were narrowed down to one. And he had already made the decision to pack up his wife, their children, and all their worldly goods and move to the Gulf Coast. The Roman empire of glory had run its course.

Courtesy of the Historic New Orleans Collection, Detail, Acc. No. 1951.74

Visiting Upriver

CHAPTER XVIII

*T*ony, true to his word, came to be with us. He and I and the children did make one trip during his stay. We visited Le Petit Versailles and spent several days with Valcour, now ailing and generally restricted by problems which he insisted were no more than the ailments of old age. It bothered me no end to see both him and Tony in less than good health, and I just couldn't imagine losing them, too. Enough is enough!

In any case, Valcour, feeling that time was running out, wanted to talk to Tony about the purchase he had made some time ago of Jefferson College. Though he had never been active in its management, he did see to the construction, and dedication to Gabi's memory, of a beautiful chapel on the spacious grounds. He was anxious to see it with Tony, and together they made the trip across the river. It was Valcour's wish that the college be donated to the Marist Fathers, in the hope that it would survive as a fine institute of higher learning.

The two of them returned quite refreshed in the late afternoon, and were unusually good company that night at dinner, as they recalled their day together.

Seeing them so happy and satisfied was special and became one of the last truly rich moments I would remember, for neither would live through another year.

CHAPTER XIX

I recall that winter as being unusually wet and cold. Valcour, although he had been bedridden for two days with a bad cold, insisted on attending Christmas Midnight Mass at St. James Church, as he had done as long as most folks could remember. Everyone advised against it and tried, to no avail, to dissuade him. Refusing to wait for a carriage and team to be readied, he threw on a cape and strode over to the stables where he insisted that his favorite stallion bc saddled. The night was getting colder by the minute, and steam could be seen coming off the horse's flanks as he galloped the seven and a half miles up river to the church.

Valcour had the horse tethered safely in a shelter nearby the church and entered in ample time for the beginning of the service. Candles illuminated the beautiful Stations of The Cross which he, Valcour, had donated to the church. Soft organ music was being played and all was serene and beautiful. At the Agnus Dei, a most glorious, golden voice suddenly filled the whole church with the beauty of song. The congregation turned toward the choir loft to see that the voice was that of Valcour's own daughter, Emma, who was standing with arms outstretched and totally inspired by the sublime moment. She, who had not sung since the night of Gabi's homecoming and tragic death, was offering this wondrous Christmas gift to her father.

Valcour was seen to grasp the edge of the pew to steady himself. Tears were pouring down his cheeks and, overcome with emotion, he appeared close to losing consciousness. He ran out the door, forgetting his cloak draped over the pew, mounted his horse and rode home in driving sleet and rain. By the time he got in the door of the Big House, he was chilled to the bone. Simon, still with him and loyal as ever, bundled him up, took him to his room and got him into bed. Valcour slept long and hard that night, but, by the next day, he had developed a persistent cough, and a fever was beginning to settle in for what looked like a long, unwelcome visit.

Each day Valcour, that tall, handsome undaunted hero of the River Road, became weaker and less and less inclined to struggle. Oddly, though, it was reported that he seemed to be somehow pleased with himself. Simon said he'd catch him with a sly smile on his blistered lips, but he wouldn't explain his thoughts to anyone. Was he seeing Gabi? Tante Jo? His dear friend Telesphore?

We would never know, for on New Years Day of 1867, Valcour took his last breath.

Tony came in time to accompany this amazing man to his eternal rest. There were none who did not acknowledge that The River Region would never be the same without him. Outstanding in life, in death he became a true legend. We would ever miss our friend the "Louis XIV of America", and know our lives were all richer for having known him.

By July of '67, Tony, too, was gone. I often picture him, Gabi and Charles in some celestial place exchanging wonderful memories of days gone by, and I envy them so much it startles me.

Courtesy of the Historic New Orleans Collection, Detail, Acc. No. 1955.45

At Home in New Orleans

CHAPTER XX

I am pleased that Jean Charles, our youngest son, has decided New Orleans is to be home. He is still young and I realize I must let him go abroad soon to complete his education, but he hopes to return one day to join his father's firm.

Marie Jo, my little bouncing doll, married her adventurous Frank and moved with him to the Big Sur country of California, where Frank had joined others in pioneering that vast area as cattle ranchers. Frank's family had been plantation owners before the war and he had always felt drawn to the land. I couldn't help but feel saddened by their move, for it was such a long, long way to go, but their daring was contagious, and I wished them well. I visited them once and found their life to be exciting and full of good things, but it is a trip I don't think will be repeated.

René, too, is doing very well as a cattle rancher. He

and Elaine often badger me to move to their home in Victoria, Texas, where they can keep an eye on me, but I cannot leave this place where so many dear ones have lived and died.

Much as I love our children, I pray that they will understand that here by the banks of the river I am at peace with my destiny, and that I shall find my share of contentment in remembering the good things ... from a joyous picnic on the levee, to a faded red rose still pressed between the pages of a book.

EPILOGUE

They are all gone now ... the century and I grow old. It is with a sense of relief that I accept the little time left for me to deal with the wild changes wrought by war, reconstruction and man's struggle on behalf of what he feels is much needed social reform. I think of history's many crusades which the noble-minded have set forth upon in the name of justice; of great words of wisdom quoted throughout the ages, and find myself ever returning to those of the Master when He reminds us that, "The poor you will have with you always ...". Indeed, it seems that Golden Ages do not flourish at a level of prevailing social equality, and a conscientious cooperation between master and slave, employer and employee, has more often than not proved to be the great catalyst for creative genius. The agony and the ecstasy ... the perpetual paradox!

Yet, something always remains from a Golden Age's cache of treasures. And so it is that I have promised myself one last stroll down that alley of magnificent oaks. I will sit on the verandah and contemplate the green swell of the levee, content in the knowledge that though life and the great river beyond continue to flow in a current of ever changing ripples, there will never cease to be passers-by who must pause in wonder at the beauty of one man's dream, and will be inspired!

The Chapel at Jefferson College by J. Frazar Smith, 1941

The End

Joanne Amort

Although born and raised in California, marriage into a coffee/cattle pioneering family in Central America resulted in 25 years residence, six children, and the remarkable experience of life in pre-revolution Nicaragua. The family returned to the USA in 1971, following Norman S. Amort's appointment as Consul General of Nicaragua in New Orleans, and ultimately settled in La Place. Joanne has been a member of the Oak Alley Foundation staff since the end of 1983.